Mason Jar
CRAFTS

Easy Projects to Make From Everyday Canning Jars

Ana Araujo

DESIGN ORIGINALS
an Imprint of Fox Chapel Publishing
www.d-originals.com

Contents

14

Jam Jar Fabric Caps

16

Basket-Style Jar Wrappers

18

Cookie Mix Jar Hats

20

Chalkboard Vinyl Name Labels

22

Decorated Drink Jars

24

Cup of Tea Time

26

Fairy Home

28

Beautiful Bird
Sewing Jar

30

Toothbrush Holder

32

Vanity Storage Jar

34

Cream and Sugar Jars

36

Succulent Vignette

38

Love Note Glitter Vases

The world of mason jars is wider than you think.

Let's talk mason jars—but I'm not talking your mother's preserves. For decades, mason jars have served all sorts of purposes, but now they have a new look in creative crafting. Whether you are planning a wedding or party, looking to make a unique handmade gift for a loved one, or aiming to spice up your home storage, mason jars fit the bill. This book provides inspiration for tons of crafts, including beautiful and even ingenious jar designs that are inexpensive and easy to make. You'll learn and use basic skills like decoupage, stenciling, and stitching while playing with different kinds of paints and spray paints. Have fun searching for the perfect embellishments for your jars from craft and fabric stores, or even hunting down vintage finds from the flea market! So grab one of these familiar glass jars off your shelf, and let's get to making something new and exciting.

Let the madness begin!

FROM THE KITCHEN OF
Susan

MASON JAR
SIZES

4 oz. quilted jelly jar

8 oz. quilted jelly jar

Small milk bottle

16 oz. regular mouth jar

16 oz. wide mouth jar

16 oz. mug jar

24 oz. wide mouth jar

32 oz. regular mouth jar

64 oz. wide mouth jar

Jar Basics

There is a wide variety of mason jar shapes and sizes, including regular and wide mouth jars, quilted and plain jars, specially shaped jars, and jars as small as four ounces and as large as one gallon. Shown in the photo at left are most of the sizes and shapes of jars used in this book. You can decide to use a different size than the one called for in the particular project you are working on, but be sure to read through the entire project before changing the jar size, as some projects do only work with certain jar sizes or size combinations.

Outside of the United States, mason jars come in metric sizes that more or less line up with the US sizes. Convert the ounces to milliliters and round off to figure out what size metric jar you should buy.

Adhesives

There are many varieties of glues and tapes to choose from. What you should use depends on the surfaces you are dealing with. Here is a quick guide for what to use where.

- **Industrial strength adhesive glue:** use to attach glass, mirrors, jar lids to jar rims, knobs of all kinds, and metal hardware.
- **3 in 1 craft glue:** use to attach trims, charms, chains, etc.
- **Hot glue:** use anywhere you want a quick-drying glue, but do not use on knobs.
- **Glue stick:** use with any kind of paper.
- **Redline adhesive tape (extra-strong double-sided tape):** use on cardstock, charms, tags, etc.
- **Foam mounting tape:** use for anything that you want raised from the surface of the jar.

Jar rim

Jar lid

Many projects reference jar lids and jar rims specifically, so keep this in mind while you are creating your jar!

Inside-the-Jar Spray Painting

Try spray painting the inside of a jar! Hold the spray paint right to the opening of the jar and spray, coating the inside of the jar. Wrap plastic wrap around the entire outside of the jar and wear gloves when doing this. If desired, carefully decoupage a paper shape inside the jar and let dry before painting.

Chalk-Finish Paint

Originally used for furniture finishing, chalk-finish paint actually works well on glass! Apply two or three coats of chalk-finish paint, depending on the effect you want. There is also a cream wax finish that is made for use with chalk-finish paint that can give your jar an antique look. These waxes come in different browns and also in clear. Once you apply it, let it dry, then buff it with a cloth.

Chalkboard Paint

Using chalkboard paint on glass can be a bit tricky. Use the following sequence, allowing the paint to dry between each layer. Start with a coat of chalkboard paint with up-and-down strokes. Add a second coat of chalkboard paint with side-to-side strokes. Finally, add a third layer of chalkboard paint with up-and-down strokes. The last step is "curing" the paint: rub a piece of white chalk all over the dry paint, and then wipe it off with a paper towel.

Jar Jewelry

Make simple jar jewelry using inexpensive hair elastics by attaching charms to the elastics with jump rings. It's an easy way to add some extra pizazz to any jar! Use two pairs of jewelry pliers to open the jump rings, spreading the jump rings apart side to side. Add charms or tags, and then close the jump rings.

Stenciling

Create a design with stickers, then block off the areas of the jar that you don't want sprayed with tightly wrapped plastic wrap. Completely cover the opening of the jar. Spray paint the jar, allow it to dry, and remove the stickers and wrap.

Scrapbook Paper and Fabric Decoupage

Follow these steps to use one solid piece of paper or fabric for your jar. Use paperweight scrapbook paper for decoupage, not cardstock—cardstock is too heavy and will not mold to the jar well.

Tissue Paper Decoupage

1| Tear crumpled tissue paper into small pieces.

2| Apply decoupage all over the jar.

3| Place one piece of tissue paper at a time on the jar to cover the whole jar, coating the paper as you go.

4| After the jar dries, apply one or two more coats of decoupage.

Fabric and Paper

1| Measure the circumference then add ⅛" (0.3cm) to that dimension. This will be the fabric/paper length.

2| Measure the jar from the lowest screw thread on the mouth of the jar to the bottom of the jar, then add ¾" (2cm) to that dimension. This will be the fabric/paper height.

3| Cut a rectangle of fabric/paper in the length and height you calculated.

4| Draw a line along the bottom edge. Snip vertical lines up about ½" (1.5cm) along the entire length of the rectangle.

5| Coat the back of the rectangle, half of the jar (circumference-wise), and the bottom of the jar with decoupage medium. Begin pressing the rectangle to the jar using a brush with more decoupage. Continue the rest of the way around the jar, applying more decoupage as you go.

6| Overlap and press down the snipped tabs on the bottom of the jar. Apply more decoupage over the jar bottom and set aside to dry.

7| Apply one or two more coats of decoupage medium to the jar, allowing each coat to dry.

4

6

Knobs

Knobs can be made from virtually anything, from real drawer knobs to repurposed beads. Just take a look in the wood, jewelry, or kids section of your local craft store, and you will find all kinds of treasures that will make good knobs.

Most knobs can be glued to the top of the jar, but if you are using a large bead, I recommend that you also use a nail for extra security. To do this, find a short nail that will fit through your bead and hammer it through the jar lid. Take the nail out and push it up through the lid from the bottom, then glue the nail head to the jar lid, taping it to keep it in place while it dries. Force glue through the hole in the bead you want to use for a knob and carefully push it down over the nail.

Jam Jar Fabric Caps

Jam jars have sported fabric caps for years, but you will love this new twist on an old favorite!

MATERIALS

- 8 oz. quilted jelly jar or 16 oz. regular mouth jar
- Cotton print fabric
- Pom-pom or lace trim
- Straight pins
- Sewing thread and needle
- Hair elastics
- Jump ring
- Wooden tag
- Embellishments: buttons, acrylic paint, punched paper tag

Instructions

1| CUT THE FABRIC. Cut a circle 6" (15cm) in diameter from your chosen fabric.

2| SEW ON THE TRIM. Pin the trim to the edge of the fabric circle and stitch it in place using a running stitch.

3| MAKE JAR JEWELRY. Make jar jewelry out of hair elastics, a jump ring, and a wooden tag (technique on page 9). Coordinate the colors of the jar jewelry with the fabric and the jam you plan to store. Embellish as desired.

4| PLACE THE FABRIC CAP. Center the fabric on top of the jar with the lid screwed on, and then stretch the hair elastics of the jar jewelry around the jar rim, securing the fabric in place.

Basket-Style Jar Wrappers

You are going to love making these basket wrappers. They are perfect in so many ways for gift-giving jams. Hand them off to a hungry friend!

MATERIALS
- 4 or 8 oz. quilted jelly jar
- Cardboard coffee cuff
- Scrapbook paper
- Spray adhesive
- Hot glue
- ⅛" (0.3cm) hole punch
- Mini brads
- Embellishments: punched paper shapes, flowers, flat-backed beads, wooden bird

Instructions

1| PREPARE THE CUFF. Pull apart a coffee cuff and lay it out flat. Glue scrapbook paper to the printed side of the cuff using spray adhesive, and then trim off the excess paper along the outside edges of the cuff.

2| GLUE THE CUFF. Wrap the cuff around the jar so it fits tightly. Hot glue the cuff closed. Remove the cuff from the jar.

3| MAKE THE HANDLES. Cut two handles from scrapbook paper and glue them back-to-back to create one sturdy handle (pattern on page 48). Punch a hole at each end of the handle and punch a hole on either side of the cuff. Attach the handle to the cuff with mini brads.

4| MAKE THE LID COVER. Trace the jar lid on scrapbook paper and cut out the circle. Place the paper on top of the jar lid and screw the lid onto the jar. You can glue the paper to the jar lid if desired.

5| EMBELLISH THE CUFF. Embellish the cuff with punched paper shapes, flowers, charms, ribbons, etc. Slip your jam jar into the completed wrapper to turn it into a basket!

FROM THE KITCHEN OF, Susan

Cookie Mix Jar Hats

MATERIALS

- 32 oz. wide mouth jar
- Glue

Halloween Witch's Hat
- Black glitter scrapbook paper
- Embellishments: tulle, leaves, feathers, crow charm, pipe cleaner

Christmas Santa Hat
- Red felt
- White fur trim
- Jingle bell

Birthday Hat
- Scrapbook paper
- Embellishments: fabric trims, tulle

Easter Bunny Ears
- White felt
- Pink scrapbook paper
- Pipe cleaner
- Embellishments: washi tape, moss, flowers, mini eggs

Cookie mix mason jars are a longtime hit on gift-giving lists, so here are some jar hat ideas for all the best holidays!

Instructions

Halloween Witch's Hat, Christmas Santa Hat, and Birthday Hat

1| START THE HAT. Cut out the hat from the main material for each hat (pattern on page 49). Roll the hat into a cone and glue it closed using the long tab. Fold under the remaining tabs.

2| FINISH THE HAT. For the Christmas Santa Hat and the Birthday Hat, glue the hat directly to the jar rim. For the Halloween Witch's Hat, make a hat brim by gluing together two scrapbook paper circles 5" (13cm) in diameter, then gluing the hat to the hat brim and the finished hat to the jar rim.

3| EMBELLISH THE HAT. Embellish the hat with the specified materials for each hat.

Easter Bunny Ears

1| MAKE THE EARS. Cut out two felt ears and two scrapbook paper inner ears (pattern on page 49). Glue a pipe cleaner to the back of each inner ear and then glue the inner ears onto the felt ears. Fold the bottom of each ear and glue them to the jar lid.

2| EMBELLISH THE LID. Cover the jar rim with washi tape. Glue embellishments to the jar lid, covering up the bottoms of the ears.

Chalkboard Vinyl Name Labels

Once you make a set of these reusable vinyl labels, they will be your go-to for any party you throw. You can make a set for a gift and include a chalk pen.

MATERIALS

- 16 oz. regular mouth jar
- Chalkboard vinyl
- Hook-and-loop tape
- Chalk or chalk marker

Instructions

1| CUT OUT THE LABEL. Cut out a name label from chalkboard vinyl (pattern on page 48).

2| CREATE THE CLOSURE. Wrap the label around the jar to check the fit, making a temporary mark where the ends overlap. Stick or sew two small squares of hook-and-loop tape to each end of the label to create the closure.

3| FINISH THE LABEL. Wrap the label around the jar, then write a name on the label using chalk or a chalk marker.

Decorated Drink Jars

Here are four different ways to drink up with mason jars! Each jar features jar jewelry and a different theme to inspire your creativity, from a first-day-of-school milk mug to a party time celebration jar.

Instructions

1| PAINT THE JAR. Spray paint the jar with your desired design and words (technique on page 9).

2| ADD JAR JEWELRY. Create jar jewelry using hair elastics, jump rings, and embellishments (technique on page 9).

Tip!

Don't have spray paint handy? You can still make a cute drink jar! Draw a small label in whatever shape you like on scrapbook paper and cut out two copies of it. Write a name or word on one copy. Glue the labels sandwiched around a hair elastic and slide the elastic onto a jar.
Quick and simple!

MATERIALS

- 16 oz. regular mouth jar, jar mug, or small milk bottle
- Plastic wrap
- Alphabet stickers
- Spray paint
- Hair elastics
- Jump rings
- Embellishments: wooden tags, charms, bows, punched paper shapes

Cup of Tea Time

This cup of tea is a tea lover's delight! Upcycle a vintage teacup and saucer to create this one-of-a-kind tea storage jar. Fill the cup with sugar cubes and you will always be ready to brew up your favorite tea.

Instructions

1| PAINT THE RIM. Spray paint the jar rim to match the cup and saucer and allow it to dry.

2| ASSEMBLE THE PIECES. Glue the teacup to the jar rim and the jar to the saucer. Allow the glue to dry overnight.

3| EMBROIDER THE HANDKERCHIEF. Fold the handkerchief into a band with a triangle point as if folding a bandana. Pin it in place and embroider the word "tea" to the front (through all layers) using a back stitch. Tie the handkerchief around the jar.

MATERIALS

o 16 oz. regular mouth jar

o Spray paint

o Vintage teacup and saucer

o Vintage handkerchief

o Glue

o Embroidery thread and needle

o Straight pins

Fairy Home

Make believe and fairies go hand in hand. And if you believe in fairies, then this adorable fairy house is for you. Just turn on the lights and the fairies are at play!

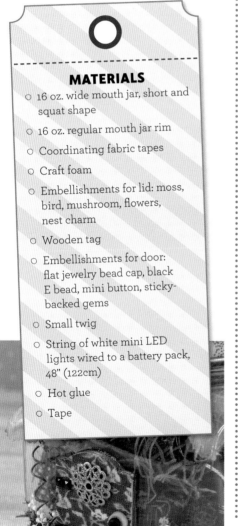

MATERIALS

- 16 oz. wide mouth jar, short and squat shape
- 16 oz. regular mouth jar rim
- Coordinating fabric tapes
- Craft foam
- Embellishments for lid: moss, bird, mushroom, flowers, nest charm
- Wooden tag
- Embellishments for door: flat jewelry bead cap, black E bead, mini button, sticky-backed gems
- Small twig
- String of white mini LED lights wired to a battery pack, 48" (122cm)
- Hot glue
- Tape

Instructions

1| ASSEMBLE THE LID. Cover the two jar rims with coordinating fabric tapes. Glue the wide mouth rim and lid together, and then glue the regular jar rim upside down on top of the wide mouth lid.

2| EMBELLISH THE LID. Cut a piece of craft foam to fit inside the regular jar rim, flush with the edge. Glue it inside the jar rim. Decorate the lid with moss, a bird, a mushroom, flowers, and a nest charm.

3| MAKE THE DOOR. Cover a wooden tag with fabric tape. Glue a flat jewelry bead cap to the center top of the tag as a window, glue an E bead on top of a mini button and glue it in place as a doorknob, and add sticky-backed gems as door hinges.

4| ATTACH THE DOOR. Attach the door to the front of the jar with glue or foam mounting tape. Hot glue moss and a flower underneath and alongside the door.

5| PREPARE THE BATTERY PACK. Cover the battery pack with fabric tape and tape it inside the bottom of the jar with the switch facing up.

6| ADD THE LIGHTS. Add some moss inside the jar. Wrap the light string loosely around a twig and mix it with more moss. Place the twig and lights inside the jar and add any more moss needed to finish filling the jar.

Beautiful Bird Sewing Jar

This jar is a must for every sewer, no matter their sewing ability. Even if you have never sewn before, you will want to make the pincushion—and it's actually quite easy to make!

MATERIALS
- 16 oz. wide mouth jar
- Embroidery floss and needle
- Lucite green felt
- Glacier gray felt
- Tangerine felt
- Straight pins
- Polyester stuffing
- Two mini buttons
- Two black seed beads
- Three sliver buttons (various sizes)
- Glue
- Cotton print fabric
- Fabric tape measure
- Sew-on button snap

Instructions

1| CUT THE PIECES. Cut out the bird pattern pieces from felt (pattern on page 48).

2| SEW THE BODY. Whip stitch the body underside to one of the body sides, starting under the neck as indicated on the pattern. Repeat to stitch the body underside to the other body side.

3| FINISH THE BODY. Whip stitch from the bird neck over the crown of the head, leaving the spine open. Stuff the bird, then stitch the rest of the body closed along the spine.

4| ADD THE TAIL. Whip stitch the two layers of the bird tail together, then stitch it to the body.

5| ADD THE WINGS. Stitch the bird wings to the bird body using the mini buttons as the wing joints.

6| ADD THE FACE. Stitch the beak in place and add the seed beads for eyes.

7| ATTACH THE BIRD. Glue or stitch the bird to the center of the jar lid and add two decorative buttons off to one side.

Tip!

To make the tape measure detail, glue a piece of fabric tape measure around the jar rim. Sew the halves of a button snap to each side of a piece of fabric tape measure, glue a silver button to one side as a decoration, and attach the piece to the jar rim as a loop for mini scissors.

Toothbrush Holder

This modified jar makes a great bathroom accent. Pick a fabric to fit your décor, add a floral jar lid, and there you have it!

MATERIALS

- 16 oz. regular mouth jar
- Cotton fabric
- Decoupage medium
- Fabric flower trim
- Glue
- Floral jar lid (with metal netting)
- Lavender spray paint
- Wooden tag (with two holes)
- Purple acrylic paint
- Hair elastic

Instructions

1| EMBELLISH THE JAR. Using two coats of decoupage medium, decoupage cotton fabric onto the jar (technique on page 11). Glue fabric flower trim around the jar just below the screw threads.

2| SPRAY PAINT THE LIDS. Spray paint the 16 oz. jar lid and the floral jar lid lavender. You do not need the 16 oz. jar rim.

3| ATTACH THE BOTTOM. Glue the painted side of the 16 oz. jar lid to the bottom of the jar—this will help prevent the bottom of the jar from getting wet.

4| CREATE THE TAG. Paint a wooden tag purple and write the word "teeth" on it. Cut a hair elastic and knot each end of it through one of the holes on the tag. Slide the tag onto the jar.

Tip!

If you don't have a floral jar lid with metal netting, make your own by hot gluing short pieces of thick jewelry wire to the underside of the jar rim.

Vanity Storage Jar

This vanity jar is super cool with its stacked structure. The pink and gold finish is great for any woman's dressing table, and you can make many to fit all your toiletries.

MATERIALS

- 4 and 8 oz. quilted jelly jars
- Pink chalk-finish paint
- Gold spray paint
- Gold metallic rub
- Gold necklace chain
- Glue
- Flat gold filigree medallion
- Large pink and gold bead
- Nail

Instructions

1| PAINT THE PIECES. Spray paint both jar rims gold. Paint one jar lid and both jars with pink chalk-finish paint. You only need one jar lid.

2| ADD THE RUB. Rub gold metallic rub onto both jars just enough to color the quilted glass lines.

3| EMBELLISH THE RIMS. Wrap and glue gold jewelry chain around both jar rims until they are completely covered.

4| ASSEMBLE THE PIECES. Glue the 4 oz. jar on top of one of the jar rims and screw it onto the 8 oz. jar. Glue the pink jar lid to the other jar rim. Then attach a filigree medallion and a large bead to the top using a nail (technique on page 13).

Tip!

Create a spray area for easy cleanup: cut open an extra large plastic garbage bag and tape it to a table, or spray small items like lids inside a large cardboard box.

Cream and Sugar Jars

Coffee time will never be the same after you put out this elegant cream and sugar set. With just a few easy steps, you can create this set for yourself and one for a friend to boot.

MATERIALS

- 4 and 8 oz. quilted jelly jars
- Silver spray paint
- Plastic wrap
- Alphabet stickers
- Sticky-backed gems or gem strips
- Crystal drawer knob
- Glue
- Recycled drink carton with spout

Instructions

1| PAINT THE JARS. Spray paint the jars silver with the words "cream" and "sugar" spelled out on them (technique on page 9).

2| ADD GEMS. Place two rows of sticky-backed gems above the word "sugar" and below the word "cream." Place four rows of gems around each jar rim.

3| ASSEMBLE THE SUGAR LID. Glue the jar lid for the sugar jar to the jar rim. Then glue a crystal knob on top of the lid.

4| ASSEMBLE THE CREAM LID. Cut out the spout and plenty of its surrounding cardboard (in one piece) from the recycled carton. Cut the cardboard around the spout to a circle the size of the jar lid by tracing the jar lid onto the cardboard. Tape off the spout and spray paint the cardboard silver. Screw it on as you would the jar lid.

Succulent Vignette

Succulents are all the rage and so fun to put on your windowsill. This clever way of showcasing a succulent will get you thinking about all the fun things you can add to the jar.

MATERIALS

- 16 oz. wide mouth jar
- 4 oz. round plastic container
- Moss
- Small twigs
- Natural decorative rocks
- Small succulent plant
- Potting soil for succulents

Instructions

1| CHECK THE FIT. Place the container into the mouth of the jar—its edges should catch on the mouth of the jar, and it should sit perfectly with the bulk of the container down inside the jar. If it doesn't fit correctly, find a different container that does.

2| EMBELLISH THE JAR. Put some rocks, twigs, and moss in the jar, only filling it about one third of the way.

3| PREPARE THE PLANT. Fill the plastic container with potting soil, add a little water, plant the succulent in the soil, and add some more moss. Set the plant in place in the jar.

Love Note Glitter Vases

This beautiful set of vases will look amazing full of flowers on a mantel. A bride would love this set to be displayed at her wedding!

MATERIALS

- Four 24 oz. wide mouth jars
- Cream/ivory chalk-finish paint
- Gold acrylic paint
- Fine gold glitter
- Decoupage medium
- Gold jewelry chain
- Gold ribbon

Instructions

1| PAINT THE JARS. Paint each jar with two coats of chalk-finish paint, allowing the paint to dry between coats.

2| TRACE THE LETTERS. Trace one letter of the word "love" on each jar with a pencil (pattern on page 49).

3| PAINT THE LETTERS. Paint each letter with gold acrylic paint. Once the paint is dry, brush decoupage medium inside the outlines of the painted letters, sprinkle glitter over the letters, and tap off the excess glitter.

4| EMBELLISH THE JARS. Cut four pieces of chain, each about 10" (25cm) long, and wrap one around each jar top, sitting them just above the lowest screw thread. Tie the chain ends together with long pieces of ribbon so that each chain sits snugly around its jar.

IDEA GALLERY

Eiffel Tower Jewelry Holder

This is the perfect way to keep track of your jewelry! Put rings around the Tower, bracelets around the jar, and other items inside the jar. Use a vintage glass plate glued to the jar as a base, and decorate the holder with washi tape and rhinestones. (8 oz. quilted jelly jar)

Simply Sweet Paper Wrap

It's so easy to make this jar! Just sew punched paper butterflies to a paper wrap. Add a paper topper to the lid, too. You can use any punched paper shape you like to theme your jar. (32 oz. regular mouth jar)

Pink Poodle Sweater Cozy

Use the arm of a pink sweater to make this cozy! Use a poodle appliqué and stitch on a piece of cording for the leash. With a running base stitch, gather the bottom of the cut sleeve to make the bottom of the cozy. (32 oz. wide mouth jar)

Hanging Bloom Jar

This spray tinted jar is great for outdoor gatherings and weddings! To make the hanger, use two D-rings and 14-gauge jewelry wire, bending the wire snugly around the D-rings and the jar mouth with needle-nose pliers. (16 oz. regular mouth jar)

Burlap Pocket Note

This jar is perfect for gift giving. Stitch the pocket to the wrap with a frayed strand of burlap. Attach a burlap flower to the jar rim, and don't forget to add a note in the pocket! (24 oz. wide mouth jar)

Woodland Tea Light

Go outside and collect nature's treasures to create this jar. Twigs, acorns, dried rose petals, leaves, flowers—anything goes! And don't forget the votive candlestick! (16 oz. wide mouth jar)

Toile Vase

This vase is so beautiful and easy to do! Spray paint the bottom third of the jar black. Decoupage toile tissue paper to the rest of the jar. (24 oz. wide mouth jar)

Toile Tea Light Votive

This tea light votive is a snap to make. Decoupage the jar rim and jar with toile tissue paper, then glue a glass votive candleholder upside down on the jar rim. What a cool effect! (4 oz. quilted jelly jar)

Cupcake Stands

Decoupage coordinating fabric on a jar and the bottom of a glass plate (such as a candle plate). Glue the fabric side of the plate to the open jar. Glue pom-pom trim around the edges. (4 and 8 oz. quilted jelly jars)

Royal Candy Dish

This dish is fit for a queen. It not only makes a great gift, but would also be a great centerpiece for wedding tables. Just glue a candy dish or candleholder to the jar rim and embellish as desired. Fill the jar and the dish with candy! (16 oz. wide mouth jar)

Baby Name Building Blocks

This is the perfect gift for a new baby's nursery! Create this piece with building blocks, scrapbook paper, paint, trims, and flowers. Glue the jar rim to the center of a candle plate, then screw the jar upside down onto the jar rim. (64 oz. wide mouth jar)

Pretty Party Favor

Favors like these are perfect for any occasion. To make the bead knobs, attach a jewelry medallion and a large bead to the jar lids using a nail. (4 oz. quilted jelly jar)

Baby Photo Nursery Jar

What a great baby shower gift—fill it with baby supplies! Decoupage fabric to the jar, then glue a baby photo to a regular jar lid and attach the lid to the front of the jar with foam mounting tape. (32 oz. wide mouth jar)

Patterns

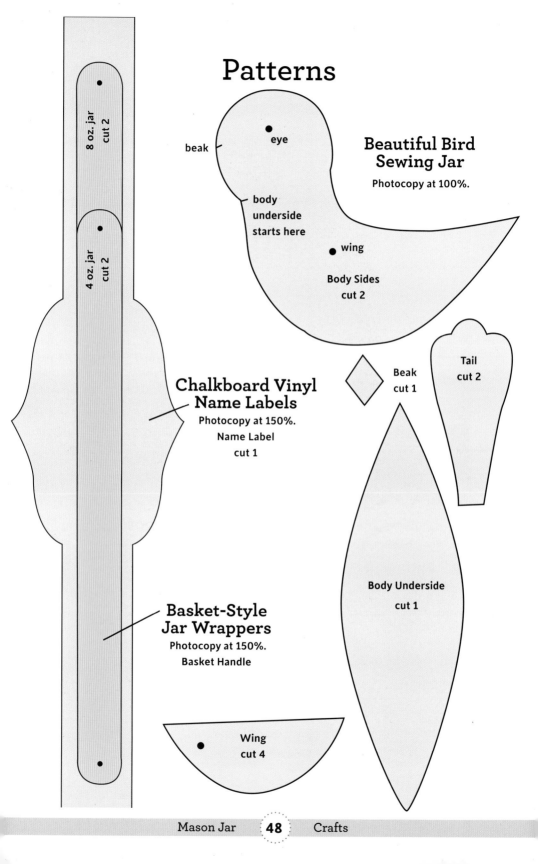

8 oz. jar
cut 2

4 oz. jar
cut 2

beak

eye

Beautiful Bird Sewing Jar

Photocopy at 100%.

body
underside
starts here

wing

Body Sides
cut 2

Chalkboard Vinyl Name Labels

Photocopy at 150%.
Name Label
cut 1

Beak
cut 1

Tail
cut 2

Body Underside
cut 1

Basket-Style Jar Wrappers

Photocopy at 150%.
Basket Handle

Wing
cut 4